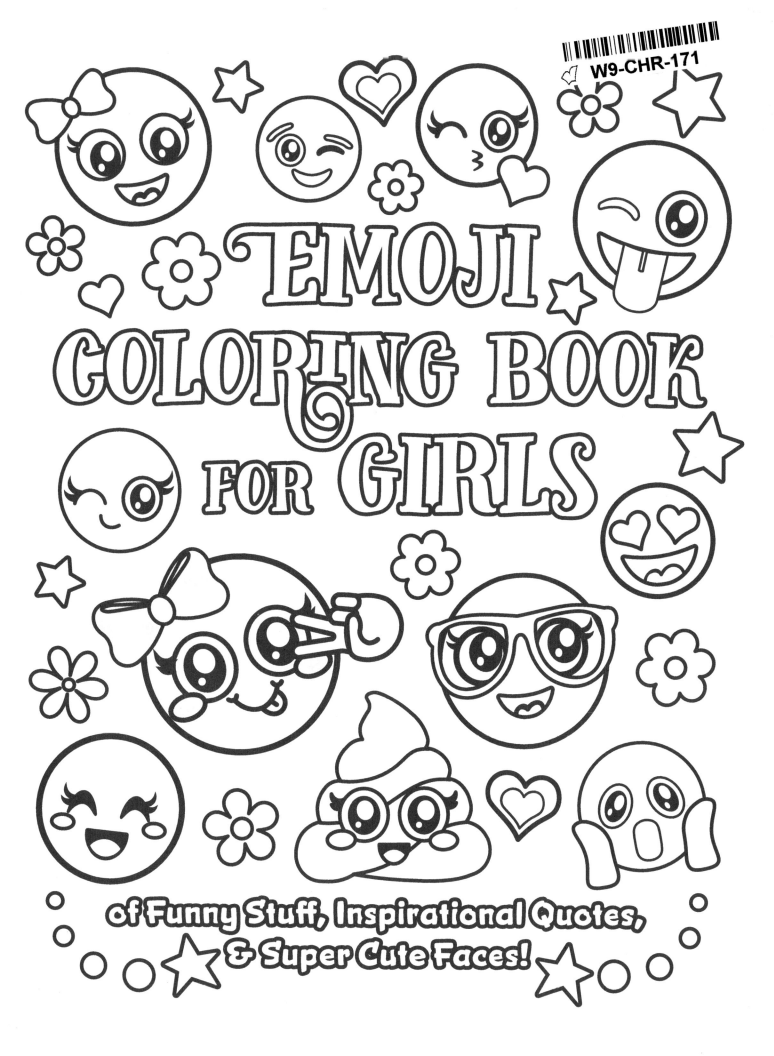

EMOJI COLORING BOOK FOR GIRLS

of Funny Stuff, Inspirational Quotes, & Super Cute Faces!

PUBLISHED IN 2017 BY
NYX SPECTRUM

PRINTED IN THE UNITED STATES OF AMERICA

I'M SO AH-DORKABLE

BFFs

TOP FIVE SNACKS

DRAW THEM!

NOW IT'S YOUR TURN!   DESIGN YOUR OWN MAGICAL MERMAID!

MONDAY ◯

TUESDAY ◯

WEDNESDAY ◯

THURSDAY ◯

FRIDAY ◯

SATURDAY ◯

SUNDAY ◯

Made in the USA
Middletown, DE
12 October 2018